LOVING THE BATTLE

Tips to Improve Your Tennis Performance

MARK TJIA

ACKNOWLEDGMENTS

I certainly would never consider my tennis career a success. After all, my goal all along since childhood was to be number one in the world. I never even came close to that. In fact, I never really made it out of the minor leagues. That can hardly be called a stellar career. I cannot, however, consider my career a failure, either, even though I never achieved my goals. Through tennis, I have been able to travel the world, meet countless wonderful people, and then meet countless more as a teacher. Through teaching, I have been able to share whatever knowledge I have accumulated with hundreds of students over the past ten years. Hopefully, through this book I will be able to reach a few more. It is my students I have to thank for providing me much of the material I used to write this book. It is also these students who have allowed me to continue making a living at this game long after I stopped playing competitively.

Specifically, I have many people to thank for helping me to write this book, because without them it would have remained only an idea in my head, to be filed away with my many other impotent ideas. With me being a total novice and a rookie author, Jo and David Black provided me invaluable expertise, advice, and inspiration, and even proofread for me. I am indebted to my coaches at TCU, Bernard "Tut" Bartzen and Karl Richter. They are two of the finest coaches in the world, and I learned more about this game from them than from anyone else. A big thank-you goes out to "Jorgy" for showing me a new approach to the mental game. Even though I only knew him for two weeks and have no idea where he is, I learned something from his unconventional approach to the mental game. From my friend Devin, I learned the value of hard work and dedication and how to get the most out of practice. If only I had met him as a child. Wanda and Neal Anderson are due my gratitude. Wanda contributed her valuable time and photography skills, and Neal deserves thanks for his advice, encouragement, and friendship. Besides tolerating all my stupid questions, my girlfriend Jenna provided me with love, support, and encouragement, and believed in me throughout this whole process. My brother Rick used his computer prowess to help me with the statistical segments of this book. Most of all, I need to thank my parents, Benny and Jenny Tjia. In addition to technical help, I am so thankful for the endless emotional and financial support they have provided me in all of my endeavors, for the countless hours spent in the car traveling to tournaments, in dirty hotel rooms, and in clubhouses during rainouts, and for sharing in the tears after those many heartbreaking losses.

TABLE OF CONTENTS

Foreword

My name is Neal Anderson and I am an avid tennis fan. As a kid, I played all the sports that my hometown of Graceville, Florida, had to offer. I was blessed to be born with lots of athleticism; even more importantly, I had a burning desire to be the best at whatever I did. Throughout grade school and high school I excelled in baseball, basketball, track, and football. Around my sophomore year in high school I started to lean toward football as what I wanted to play in college. I was fortunate enough to receive scholarship offers from just about every major university in the country. I ended up attending the University of Florida. After having a successful college career, I was drafted in the first round by the Chicago Bears of the NFL. I played eight years in Chicago, 1986–1994, before retiring as the Bears' second all-time leading rusher, behind the late Walter

Payton. My goal was to play eight years and then to retire healthy, and it worked just as I had planned. Although this has nothing to do with football or tennis, I have to mention that I also received my degree in public relations from the University of Florida. If I didn't mention it, my mom would roll over in her grave.

Now that I am on the subject of my mom, I will tell you about my initial interest in tennis. While I was in Chicago, my mom, Dorothy Anderson, died after a battle with Hodgkin's disease. As a tribute to her, I decided to endow a scholarship in her name to the women's tennis program at the University of Florida. My primary reason for choosing women's tennis was because of my respect and admiration for their legendary coach, Andi Brandi. The work ethic and self-discipline that he and his teams displayed were traits that I thought kids should have instilled in them. Through my friendship with Andi and some of his players, I decided to give tennis a try. I remember sitting in the stands, watching the matches and thinking, "How can they miss a court that is so big or hit the ball in the net that is so low?" To me, a big court + a low net = easy game. Once I finally put a racket in my hand and got out on the court, I realized just how wrong I was. It seemed as though the net grew and the court shrunk.

This is when I decided to get some instruction. My first instructor was Coach Andi Brandi. He was probably overly qualified for someone with my lack of tennis skill, so I was very happy to say the least. Andy worked with me for a few weeks and got me off to a good start. I set up a practice schedule and I also decided to start playing some matches. For someone who had never picked up a racket as a kid, I progressed rather quickly. Luckily enough, some pretty good players were willing to play with me. I worked extremely hard so that I wouldn't bore my friends who hit with me. As I started to improve, I noticed that not as many people wanted to play anymore and many of my phone calls were not being returned. At first I was upset that these people would play me when I was terrible, but as soon as I started to improve, they developed these mysterious injuries or somehow misplaced my phone number, which is listed in the club directory.

My first real test came when I played a match against a female teaching pro. What I didn't realize was that she had also played professionally. We went out to play a friendly match, and I proceeded to get spanked 6-0, 6-0. Even though the score was as bad as it could possibly be, I felt pretty good because we had some very competitive points; she just happened to win **all** of them. For the most part, her strategy was to give me another ball and another opportunity to hang myself, and I usually obliged. For some reason, I thought that a rematch sounded like a good idea. When I got to the net to shake hands and congratulate her on a good match, I happened to add that if we played again, I thought that I would win. This statement seemed to rub my opponent and a friend of hers the wrong way. Now as I look back, I actually understand why they felt the way they did, because most people would have been distraught or at least a little more humble after losing in straight sets at love. For those of you who don't know me, I am very, very competitive, to say the least. I am a true believer in "Where there is a will, there is a way." What I do know is that no one on planet Earth has a stronger will than I do. My opponent and her friend did not see this as me being ultra-competitive, but instead they saw my comments as insulting. One word led to another, and it was capped off by me being told that my statement was "asinine and ignorant." I was told that my beating her was the equivalent of them trying out for and making the team for the Chicago Bears. As I left the court, I vowed to myself that this was not the end. When I got home I wrote the words "asinine and ignorant" on a piece of paper and placed it where I would see it daily. My next order of business was to find a teaching pro who could help me. I use the phrase "order of business" because this was now my new job.

In my search for a pro, the name that kept coming up was Mark Tjia from the 300 Club. I had never heard of Mark, or of the 300 Club, but I decided to give him a try. After setting up and taking my first lesson, I knew that I had made the right choice. For a few months, Mark and I worked steadily on making me a better player to get me ready for my big rematch. After a few months of training, I made the call to set up the match. Unlike the first match, this time I had to pay for an hour and a half lesson to play against the pro. There wasn't much conversation during the warm-up period or during the changeovers. The atmosphere had the intensity of a playoff game which I liked. When the final point had been played, I was victorious in straight sets 6-2, 6-3. All the trash talk that I had planned got pushed aside, as victory was sweet enough all by itself. I even decided against giving the young ladies the free-agent forms from the Chicago Bears, even though I had been carrying them around in my tennis bag in anticipation of this day.

Although my big match was now over, I was having fun with this game, so I decided to continue playing tennis. Unfortunately, or fortunately, depending on how you look at it, nothing that I do is just for fun. Fun for me is improving and trying to be the best that you can be. So I set some tennis goals that I shared with Mark. One of my goals was to be the #1 player in the 40s age bracket in the state. Another goal was to beat Mark in three years. In regards to beating Mark, when I told him about it, he thought it was hilarious. At least he didn't think that it was "asinine and ignorant." He did, however, tell me in no uncertain terms that it would never happen. His reasons were: 1) He was way too good to let that happen ; 2) If I trained the way I said I was going to train, basically three to four hours a day, I was going to injure myself. As the third year was approaching, I realized that Mark was right on both accounts. He was too good for me and I could not seem to stay healthy. I was having a hard time dealing with the fact that after all of those years of staying healthy playing the rough and tough game of football, the seemingly docile game of tennis was kicking my butt. My injuries ranged from ankle to knee to back to elbow to shoulder. I have since developed a huge respect for tennis for both the physical and the mental aspects that it entails.

Now let's get to this book. When Mark told me that he was thinking about writing a book, I really never thought he would get past the "thinking about it" stage. One day, to my surprise, Mark handed me a rough draft of his book. When I started to read it, I was surprised at how good it was and how smooth it read. One part in particular seemed to speak directly to me. It talked about how winning should be your intention, but should not receive your attention while you play. I had been doing it 100 percent backward, because winning received all my attention while I played. In all of those years playing football, I never worried about the score or the game clock. I was always too busy concentrating on the next play, like how many steps I needed to take or what route I was going to run. I never wanted the game to end. I didn't want that clock to run out. I figured the more time that was left on the clock, the worse beating I could give to the other team's defense. After reading Mark's book, I realized that I was not thinking the same way in tennis. I would often think about the score and how close to the end of the game, the set, or the match it was while I was still playing. Armed with this new information, I proceeded to go out and play a great match the following day. This simple thought seemed to free up my swing, and served to put my attention where it should have been in the first place, on each individual shot. The bottom line is that this book promises to be both educational and entertaining for anyone who likes the game of tennis. I hope you enjoy reading this book as much as I did and maybe even play a little bit differently because of it.

Chapter One

MY STREET CRED

Okay, so if you are reading this right now, I can assume that you are either a close personal friend or you are at your wit's end trying to find a solution to the mental lapses on the court that you believe are holding your tennis game back. One of my coaches once told me in my early days of junior tennis in Florida that 90 percent of the game of tennis takes place from the shoulders up. As a junior, I never quite realized the significance of this statement. I am not sure how you assign a percentage to something like this, but I am here to say that the point is , a significant portion of this game has to do with that mental side of tennis, perhaps more so than any other sport, with golf running a close second. Still, even in golf, decisions are not being made in seconds or fractions of a second. Nevertheless, it is not my intent to debate the difficulty level of certain sports. The physical skills that tennis requires—speed, hand/eye coordination, endurance, precision timing—combined with the mental skills involved make it one of the more difficult sports in which to really excel and especially to become a professional. I played many sports in my younger days. Mostly though, I dedicated my life to the sport I love…and hate, tennis. I played almost every day from the age of eight until I retired from professional tennis at the age of 24 almost ten years ago (wow! has it been that long?). Growing up in Gainesville, Florida, I was always among the top 10 or 15 juniors in the state. I played nationals every summer and was generally considered a pretty good player by people who knew the game. I was undersized (I guess I still am, although significantly heavier now) when I entered Texas Christian University on a tennis scholarship in 1988. I still have my college program from my sophomore year, which lists me as five foot six inches and 131 pounds. I was not much heavier than that when I turned pro after graduating in 1992. On limited funds, I managed to play satellites and challengers around the world for two and one-half years. For those of you who don't know, satellites and challengers are the minor leagues of pro tennis. Almost all of the pros you see playing on TV today had to spend the early part of their careers toiling on this part of the circuit, playing for little money in the most obscure places on the planet and trying to earn enough ATP points to make the jump to the big tournaments. The quality of tennis in these tournaments is not far from what you witness on TV, just in case any of you ever have a chance to watch any of these events in or near your hometown. If you think you are dealing with pressure when you play your local club matches, try playing in a godforsaken third-world country where the outcome of the match determines whether you get enough prize money and ATP points to move on to the next tournament so you can continue to pursue your dream. There are literally thousands of damn good tennis players around the world chasing their dream under conditions like these. I learned an immense amount about myself and my mental toughness by playing under these conditions. I also learned a ton from playing college tennis where my best friends, my brothers, were counting on me to contribute to their victory. Many of you find yourselves under the same conditions playing in your local league matches. This can be a different kind of pressure depending on how you interpret it, but it can be just as daunting nonetheless. Pressure can do strange things to people. In reality, pressure is neither positive nor negative, it is just there, and how you perceive it will help determine how you deal with it. If you perceive it to be a negative thing and fear it, chances are you will not perform well in those conditions. In contrast, if you get excited by the pressure and see it as a challenge, you will generally perform well. Clutch players like Michael Jordan thrive in pressure situations because they actually enjoy these situations. This is a key element for success, and I will address this again later. There are many different reasons why tennis is such a difficult and therefore frustrating sport.

As a tennis coach for the better part of ten years, I often hear how a particular junior is so talented and how they are going to be a top pro one day. I never fail to find this an amusing statement. There is no way to tell how someone will do in the long term. You don't know how people will react. There are so many factors involved in becoming a successful tennis player besides being supremely talented. There are countless stories of child prodigies who just never really made it for one reason or another. Talent is only a small part of the equation. In the NBA, high school kids are drafted and paid millions of dollars based purely on their physical talent. This occurs in baseball as well. Tennis is much more mental than those sports. Talent alone will not get you to the promised land.

I struggled with the mental side of the game for many years and still do today. It is always an ongoing struggle, and impossible to master, but that doesn't mean you shouldn't stop trying. Everyone is susceptible to a lapse or choke or mental breakdown. Just ask former Wimbledon champion Jana Novotna, who lost in the 1993 Wimbledon final after leading Steffi Graf 6-7, 6-1, 4-1 (40-15). She had a mental collapse, spraying balls everywhere, including even an easy overhead into the stands. It can and has happened to the best of us. Our goal is to limit the times we lapse, and perhaps even win in spite of those lapses. My goal is to help you enjoy competing and thereby help you perform well under stressful situations, and hopefully give you more satisfactory results.

So what does all this mean for you? I have spent the better part of 25 years playing, working, analyzing, scouting, teaching, living, sleeping, and drinking tennis. I like to consider myself of average intelligence (I hope). I don't have a PhD. My bachelor's degree is actually in marketing, about which I couldn't tell you two things. I don't know a lot about many things, but I am supremely confident that I do know this game. It is all I know and have known. The amount of time I have spent on this game would easily equal eight PhDs. I have never written anything of significance in my life. In fact, the last time I wrote anything more than two pages in length was in a college business class years ago. I felt compelled, however, to write down my own thoughts, unique as they are, in the hopes of helping some of you achieve better results and more enjoyment from this game we all love.

I have never read, or rather finished, any book on the mental side of tennis. Such books might have been very good, but I could never relate to them. Everything sounded good in theory; but, being of average intelligence, I could not translate all the psychological mumbo jumbo to what was actually happening on the court. Making the jump from theory to reality was always a big leap for me. When I was a junior, my mother, bless her heart, in an attempt to cure my mental weaknesses sent me to the sports psychologist at the local university. We spent numerous sessions at a cost of $50 per hour doing everything from talking, to hypnosis, to breathing exercises, to trying to control my tightness and nervousness in certain stages of the match. I think the fact that the psychologist was not a competitive tennis player made it hard for me to relate to him. I just don't think you can understand what players are feeling unless you have felt it yourself. That's when I think theory goes out the window. I remember him telling me to visualize a "happy place" to calm my thoughts as I pinched my fingers together. During the match as I was feeling myself get tight, I was supposed to pinch my fingers together and revisit my calm feelings elicited by visiting my "happy place." Are you done laughing yet? Needless to say, this didn't work for me. It was through the accumulation of all my tennis experiences—the wins, the losses, triumphs, and disappointments—that I finally began to understand the mental approach that worked best for me. The old cliché "if I knew then what I know now" holds very true for me. Because I was of such small physical stature and physically unimposing, I had to learn to try to gain a mental advantage over my opponent instead of relying on having a physical one. Unfortunately for me, I never mastered the mental side of the game, but I did get a whole lot better at it. It is my hope that my experiences as a player, and later as a coach on the WTA tour, and currently as a coach for tournament and recreational players of all ages and levels at a private club in Florida can help your mental approach to the game. I guess you could say that this is sort of a blue-collar and practical way of dealing with common mental mistakes. It is my wish to share with you my philosophies on the mental game that have worked

for me in the hopes that they may help you as well.

Chapter Two

COMPETITION

What does it mean to be a competitive person? Many of the problems people have in their mental games stem from their true competitive or noncompetitive nature. Being competitive is not as easily defined as one would think. Tennis is one of the ultimate competitive games. It is combative. It is no different in attitude from sports such as boxing, wrestling, fighting, or chess. It is *mano a mano*, one on one, me against you, one winner and one loser every single time. It takes a big man or woman to walk up to the net after two hours of battling and look your opponent in the eye while you shake his/her hand and say "Good match, you were better than me. You outplayed me, **no excuses**." I would be a rich man if I had a dime for every time I heard a student tell me after a match, "I am not making any excuses, **but**…"

This type of pressure differs from team sports such as football and basketball. Even team tennis is not the same because ultimately, tennis is still an individual sport even though it can be played in a team format. You still win or lose individually. In team sports, the loss and therefore the blame can be shared. I remember that as a child, I never had the same nervousness before a soccer game that I felt before my tennis tournaments. Soccer games were just pure action and adrenaline. In tennis matches, even before the matches—and sometimes days before—I felt excitement accompanied by nervousness, apprehension, and a myriad of other feelings. Both soccer and tennis meant a lot to me. I wanted to win equally as bad in both sports. Now that brings me to my original point. What does it mean to be competitive? You must be a competitive person to excel at this sport. You must love to win, and hate to lose, but more importantly, you must **love the battle**. To be truly competitive, you must not only endure but enjoy the struggle to win. The highs and lows that you encounter in a closely contested match are what intrigue and excite the true competitor. Not only does he not shy away from that struggle, he seeks it out. Being really competitive goes far beyond just wanting to win. The competitor loves the battle—that is, the challenge and struggle to prevail—more than the win itself. The journey actually excites him more than the destination.

I encounter this every day in the local leagues that I coach. One lady complained to me one day about the partner I had put her with. She told me, "I want to play with a stronger partner. I want to play lower in the lineup, because I am a competitive person. I take my tennis seriously and I like to win!" Oh really? Everyone likes to win. Everyone is not competitive. Do you know of anyone who likes to lose? The desire to win doesn't alone make you competitive. The competitive person would welcome the challenge of playing higher or lower, for that matter. He would also welcome the challenge of playing with a weaker partner, especially in a team setting. As simple as this sounds, this concept is exactly the problem for many of you. The focus on winning is too strong. Total preoccupation with the outcome of the match can actually suppress your performance and make that with which you have preoccupied yourself more difficult to achieve. The pitfalls of this mentality are numerous and will be addressed later again.

When I was nine years old, I remember playing this kid in the finals of a ten and under tournament in Amelia Island, Florida. I still remember every detail like it was yesterday, right down to the actual court. It was at the same facility where the WTA Tour's Bausch and Lomb Championships are now held. Anyway, I was losing 4-1 in the first set when my stomach became upset. After a couple of timeouts, there was still a sharp pain in my stomach, and I had exceeded my injury timeouts. The tournament referee, who was on site, was prepared to call the match on account of an illness retirement. My opponent, who had been extremely patient and genuinely concerned, said, "Why don't we stop, go to lunch, wait a couple hours, and come back later in the day and continue then?" Keep in mind that this was a totally original idea coming from a ten-year-old. Needless to say, I was very surprised at the generous offer and we agreed to come back a couple of hours later. I ended up barfing my lunch up in the car and I didn't continue the match, but that is beside the point. His offer was genuine and not influenced by any grown-ups. There was always the possibility that I might have come back feeling great and perhaps beaten him. He was risking interruption of his rhythm or concentration because he loved to play and wanted the challenge even though he might have risked a loss. To that little kid, winning was not as important as playing and competing. If the tables were turned, I know that as a nine-year-old, I would not have made the same offer. I would have taken the retirement and scampered out of there with my win and my trophy.

Six years later, I was scheduled to play the same kid in the finals of a tournament in my hometown. Actually, it was held at my home club, the club where I still teach today. I had benefited from a default in the semifinals and didn't have to play, while he had won a long, tough match in the other semi. I remember we had rain that weekend and matches were backed up. I had only played one match that day and he had played twice. The most matches you were required to play in one day was two. It was late Sunday night and they were still engaged in the long three-setter in the other semifinal. The final was scheduled for the next day, Monday. I could not miss school, so I elected to default the final. I informed the tournament director that I would be defaulting. As my parents and I were driving from the club, I saw in the rearview mirror this kid literally chasing our car with his hands frantically waving above his head. You would have thought he was flagging down an ambulance or something, the way he approached our car. It was the same kid I was scheduled to play in the final. He had just won his semifinal match and found out from the director that I was going to default the next day's final, making him the champion.

"What are you doing?" he gasped when he got to our window.

"I can't miss another day of school tomorrow, so I'm going to default," I replied.

"Then we can play it today."

Startled, I replied, "What? Are you sure? You just played twice in a row to my once."

"It's better than not playing at all. You're my best competition here. We can play now."

Maybe he made this self-sacrificing offer because he knew he was going to kick my ass anyway, but I like to think that he just had an unusual love for competition and for playing tennis. As I recall, we had a fairly close match; it was not a walkover for him. I have always remembered these two events like they happened yesterday, because they were so unique. I have never encountered another attitude quite like this in all my years of competitive tennis. In both instances, this kid played these matches at a considerable disadvantage to himself even though he could have been automatically declared the champion of the tournament by simply not playing at all. This is a true example of competitiveness. His love of competition was stronger than his love of winning. They are not one and the same. How many of you as grown adults would have done the same? I see many of the reverse examples today. "Is he allowed to go to the bathroom? Don't I get point penalties for that? How many minutes does he have until I get a default?" I hear it from children and parents alike. I was the same way as a child. I just wanted the win. I wanted the easiest draw, anything, because I just wanted the win. By the way, the kid in the story is Jim Courier, two-time French Open Champion, two-time Australian Open champion, U.S. Open and Wimbledon finalist, and former world #1. Even then as a ten-year-old kid, he had an unusually strong competitive spirit. As a pro, he was known not for his talent, but for his feistiness and grit on the court—his heart. This is a quality that is essential in developing mental fortitude.

Love the Battle. You must enjoy the challenge that different situations present, even more than the outcome itself. Find the challenge in every match you play. Play everyone. If an inferior player asks you to play, don't avoid him. Beat him as badly as you can. Play two sets instead of one to work on your concentration and focus. The challenge here is in maintaining your concentration and playing the fewest loose points possible. If you are capable of winning 6-0, then do it.

Don't win 6-2 simply because you have superior physical skills. We have already established the importance of the mental game. Work on it, practice the mental game. It is the most important part of the game and yet usually the least practiced. Practice it as you would your serve, forehand, or any other stroke. Too often I see players win with 70 percent concentration simply because they are better tennis players. What is the challenge in that? If you do this, you will have achieved nothing. You will have just wasted your time. If you're playing with a weaker partner in doubles, then accept that as your challenge. Concentrate to execute better to reduce your preventable mistakes and help to elevate your partner's game. There is a challenge to be found in every match or practice. Find it and work to overcome that challenge.

Chapter Three

INTENTION vs. ATTENTION

After college, I played a number of smaller professional tournaments called satellites and challengers. At that time, satellites consisted of four tournaments in a row in the same general area. Each tournament lasted one week, and you were required to play all of them in order to have a chance to earn ATP points, which determined your world ranking. There was plenty of free time if you lost in the early rounds, because you had to wait around for the next tournament to start the following week. This could become quite expensive as well; four weeks in a motel can drain a pocketbook pretty quickly. The prize money for these satellites was a joke. It would more or less average out to less than $100 for every match won. You played one match per day, and it was easy to lose in the early rounds as generally everyone in them had world rankings. Translation: everyone was damn good. You don't fly around the world and play these things unless you have some game. There were even separate qualifier tournaments held a few days before to see which lower-ranking participants could qualify to enter. Well, one time a college teammate of mine, Tony Bujan, and a friend, Frederik Bergh (NCAA singles finalist in '94), set off to play a satellite in Mexico. The tournaments were located in Tijuana, Ensenada, and one other city I can't remember now, but they were all located somewhere in the Baja peninsula, south of California. An acquaintance of Tony's knew someone who had an available condo on the beach about 30 minutes from Ensenada. It was a very nice place, and they agreed to let the three of us stay there free for two weeks during the satellite. There was only one condition. A man named Jorgan (we called him Jorgy) was to accompany us and help us with our mental games. Apparently, Jorgy and friends were somehow connected with the Church of Scientology. They wanted to try new mental training techniques on professional athletes, particularly tennis players. In return for the free accommodations, we agreed to participate in Jorgy's exercises for a couple of hours each day once we were out of the tournament. It was a no brainer for broke, aspiring 21-year-old tennis pros trying to make the big time. The exercises were grueling and mostly absurd, but I did learn some valuable things that I will share with you.

The jest of these exercises was to achieve the ever-elusive "zone." This is a state in which an athlete is clicking on all cylinders and just can't seem to do anything wrong. When a tennis player has entered it, the ball seems huge and slow. To a basketball player, the hoop seems huge. It was Jorgy's contention that it was possible to enter the zone every time you played. I am not sure you could do that, but I understood the message of intense concentration. By the way, I am not suggesting that you do any of these exercises; I am merely describing them to you for illustrative purposes. It just so happened Tony made it to the finals that week and Fredrik and I did not fare so well, so we had the most spare time, and thus participated in the mental drills the most. In one exercise, Frederik and I sat in wooden dining-room chairs for two hours.

We were not to move, talk, or open our eyes, but above all, we were not allowed to fall asleep. This was extremely difficult. You would be surprised how much concentration was required to ignore the pain in our asses from sitting for so long and the effort that it took just to resist falling to the floor in a deep slumber. In another exercise, we faced one another in the same chairs and stared at each other for 15 minutes. Anytime we laughed (which we did a lot of), smiled, or changed expression, we had to start over. This exercise was particularly difficult because it required extreme concentration and control over your thoughts. We did other drills that basically dealt with concentration.

Eventually we made it to the practice court in an effort to transfer our newfound skills in concentration to the tennis court. We started with the universal cross-court forehand drill. We were trying to achieve the same state of mind we had during the drills by blocking out external thoughts or stimuli. We concentrated on just picking the target, watching the ball, and rhythm hitting, trying to make each shot the same as the last.

The goal was to get to the point where we no longer were aware of anything but the ball; even to the point that we no longer knew whether we had hit 20 or 80 balls in a row. I never quite got to that level, but what I came away with from these drills is the need to block out external stimuli as best you can. The only thing that is important when you are playing is what is happening between the lines at that time. That means that the couple talking loudly two courts down, or the gentlemen sitting too close to the court, or the reputation of your opponent, or even your burning desire to win cannot be allowed to distract you. These are all external stimuli and largely irrelevant. I know this is easier said than done and sounds good in theory but is hard to translate to reality on the tennis court. I agree, but we all possess this ability. Mentally, I compare it to driving your car in a huge downpour of rain where you can barely see the road in front of you. You are driving down the highway in this deluge, with heavy traffic on all sides. Your conversation drops off; no longer are you aware of what song is playing on the radio or thinking of what you are preparing for dinner. Your concentration has increased, and the road in front of you is the only thing that is important at that moment. If you had to do this for two hours straight, you would be tired, more so than had you driven two hours under perfect conditions. My point is: don't put your mind on cruise control while playing. Focus between the lines, and if you do that, you won't be aware of that loud couple or people clapping on mistakes or any other things that bother you when you are playing. If you are able to achieve this state, you ought to be at least a little mentally drained when you come off the court regardless of the score. Again, this takes practice and discipline. One coach told me that the average attention span for an adult is seven minutes. After teaching for ten years, I believe it is probably less than that. That is why concentrating for an entire match (two or three hours) takes a conscious effort and practice. I find that when I play matches now, which I don't do a whole lot of anymore, that is what suffers. My physical skills are usually fairly adequate, but my concentration is not because I have not practiced it.

A more common but less obvious distraction can be your total preoccupation with the outcome of the match—basically, with winning. With the wrong approach, your intense desire to win and hatred of losing can actually be detrimental. Again, if you are truly competitive and are caught up in the struggle and process of playing, your intense desire to win can help pull you through, almost willing you to victory. However, if your primary focus is on the result itself and not on the process of getting you there, that desire can seriously hinder your performance. For me to say, "Don't worry about the score!" is unrealistic. Of course you have to be aware of the score. After all, there is a reason why you are fighting tooth and nail out there. But **let the fight itself be your focus and not the outcome**. In other words, **let your INTENTION be on winning, not your ATTENTION.** Don't be distracted by your focus on the end result. Concern yourself only with the things you can control. You cannot always control whether you will win or lose a match. Your opponent or even your partner has a large say as to who wins and who loses. You can, however, control the quality of your performance in spite of your opponent or partner. A partner's play and attitude can definitely help you to play better, but their poor play can only make you play worse if you let it.

Don't try to skip steps to get to your goal. Although the **intent** or ultimate goal is to emerge victorious, focus on the steps that are necessary to get you there: that is, concentrating on the task at hand, moving your feet, watching the ball etc. Play positively; you cannot play in fear of not achieving your goal. Think about **performing**, as an actor performs onstage. An actor tries to give the best performance that he can at that moment in time. He is not concerned with the consequences of that performance while he is giving it, whether it is bad reviews, lost auditions, a potential Oscar, or the like. When they allow that kind of negative thinking to enter their minds, they essentially choke. Good actors don't think like this, yet we as tennis players do that all the time. When you perform to your ability, you will generally defeat the people who are not as good as you and lose to the people who are better than you and performed better that day. What more can you ask for? We tend to become our own worst enemy and introduce our own obstacles to achieving our full potential because of our emphasis on the consequences of our performance rather than on the performance itself.

Chapter Four

THIS IS A GAME

43

There are many different aspects and therefore many different potential problems to consider when discussing the mental game. In addition, people are different and will respond differently to similar situations. I have tried to identify some of the common problems that people complain about and that I have also personally struggled with at times.

NERVOUSNESS AND PRESSURE

Many of the people I teach, especially at the club level, play so well in practice and in practice matches, but play far worse when playing a match of consequence such as in a league or tournament match. The only logical reason why they can play well in one setting and so poorly in another is because of their mental approach to the different situations. My old college coach, the legendary Bernard "Tut" Bartzen, always told me to "play like you practice and practice like you play." If you practice one way and play matches with a different mindset it transforms your physical play, and, therefore, all your practice is useless as you are playing a totally different game. We had a term to describe guys like this on our team in college. We called them "practice players." Needless to say, they rarely saw the match court. It is a derogatory term with which you do not want to be labeled. Often when teaching my clinics, I will keep score during the drills to make the drill a little more interesting. Students always try their best to win those games, but they are not consumed with the end result. They know that we are going to play another game right after that one, and another one after that. This is where the true competitive nature of the player is really evident. Students tend to play well in these drills, because their focus is in the present. They are not getting caught up in the final result; they are playing in the *present*. Players should try to carry this same mentality into their match play. Once again, all this sounds great in theory, but how do you put it into action?

As mentioned earlier, make sure your emphasis is on your performance and not overly directed at your result. Let the results work themselves out based on the quality of your play. Remember, the quality of your play is the only thing you have 100 percent control over, not winning or losing. Remember that regardless of the perceived magnitude of the match, whether it is your club championships or the deciding match in league play, you will **always** have another opportunity regardless of the outcome. This will help reduce your self-imposed pressure. One of the great things about tennis is that there is always tomorrow, next week, or next year. There will always be another tournament or league match to redeem yourself if things do not go as planned this time around. Even at the pro level, there are always more matches to be played the following week. There is not the one all-important match that is life or death. I always get nervous watching Olympic athletes compete in their respective sports. Now that is pressure. Watching an athlete have one single routine or race determine their success or failure for the next four years can be excruciating, even for the casual observer. Tennis is not like that. You will always have another chance. Keep it in perspective. Remember that you **play** tennis, with emphasis on the word **play**. It is never life or death. No matter what level you play, in the end it is a game that you elect to pursue simply because you enjoy playing. Don't lose sight of that.

This truth really hit home with me years ago when I played a couple of tournaments in Bangladesh. If you don't already know, Bangladesh is one of the poorest countries in the world. I remember walking from the hotel (and I use that word very loosely, as most westerners would hardly call it that) to the tennis courts and being mobbed by people asking for money. Little did they know that I was a struggling tennis pro and therefore by definition had none. Nevertheless, on the way to the courts, I saw what looked to be a mangled mass of flesh on the side of the road. My curiosity got the best of me. As I crossed the road to inspect it more closely, I barely recognized it to be a human being—a beggar, in fact. He had no legs and not much of a torso either. This poor chap's plight made the obstacles that I was about to face on the court and on the circuit virtually irrelevant. The tennis stadiums where we played our matches in Bangladesh were very nice, with large seating capacity for fans (of which there were none) and nice court surfaces. However, once I stepped just outside of the complex, there was poverty everywhere. Suddenly, my struggles on the court paled in comparison to the struggle for life that was occurring outside the stadium walls. Even though tennis was my life and my income depended on my results, somehow the overhead I had just netted on break point didn't seem quite as catastrophic as it should have, I guess. I remember that a significant number of ball boys had dark rings under their eyes, which I was later told was a sign of malnutrition. The point I am trying to make is that tennis is never life or death regardless of what level you play. That is certainly true for all you club players out there. The sooner you realize that and begin to enjoy the moment and the challenge of competition, the sooner you will excel when the spotlight is on you. The great players in all sports play better in matches than in practice and not the reverse. The great ones enjoy those situations. Michael Jordan wants to have the ball when the game is on the line because he enjoys those moments, as tense as they are. It excites him. He also always believes he will be successful in those moments, even though he is not. Even when he misses to lose the game, he will want the ball again given the same conditions in the very next game. That is confidence. Believe in yourself. Want the ball! At the same time, you have to realize that disappointments will happen too. That is what makes competition so much fun. You have to have lows to know how sweet the highs feel. To learn to excel in these situations, you must learn to enjoy these situations when the match gets close. The worst feeling to have on the court is not wanting to play. That is, hoping your opponents hit to your partner instead of you, or hoping your opponents miss first so you won't have a chance to miss. **Want the ball!** You are there to play. Execute as you know you can and let the results be as they may.

I finally learned to play well under these situations when I did exactly that. I used to dread these tight matches, tiebreakers, etc. I remember feeling like I was trying to survive these situations instead of confronting them and embracing them. I began to concentrate on performing beautiful, well-played points and began thinking positively. It is so important to think positively. It is equally important to be sure you know exactly what that means. One of the sports psychologists in my childhood once used this example to illustrate this point: If I repeatedly told you, "Don't think about bears!" you would have a hard time not thinking about bears. That is how our mind works. If I had not introduced that thought to you at all, there is a very good possibility that bears would never have entered your thoughts, but since I told you not to do it, it is hard to get rid of that image. In tennis, if you tell yourself to not miss, or make a mistake, or double fault, you have just introduced the possibility of those things actually occurring. This is what we call choking. I am reminded of the scene in Austin Powers III, where Powers is trying to avoid staring at a large mole on a man's face and ultimately he cannot help himself from pointing at it and screaming, "Moley, moley, mole!", only because he is trying **not** to notice it. We have all done it. Well not that, but choking. It is an awful feeling. You can literally feel when you are doing it. If it weren't so frustrating, it would be comical. How about this one: Your opponent barely gets a ball and is way off the court and all you have to do is put it anywhere in the court, and you hit it out or dump it in the net because all you had to do was not miss it. You are telling yourself to "just make it" or "not miss it," and that is negative thinking. A friend of mine, Neal Anderson (former All-Pro running back for the Chicago Bears and a current avid tennis player) and I were discussing this concept one day when he told me what his sports psychologist with the Chicago Bears told him: "Picture three Sunkist lemons against a black backdrop. Visualize the yellow skin with the green Sunkist stamp on it, dew dripping down the dimpled surface…Now, don't think about them anymore. It's not easy to do, is it? Now picture three green Chiquita bananas against a green backdrop and carefully visualize every detail.

Suddenly you're not concerned about the lemons anymore." The point is, you cannot easily remove a thought from your head, but you can replace it. Let's get back to our example of the open court with the opponent out of play. Hit the ball as you have the entire point, don't hit the ball any differently just because your opponent is off the court. The only difference now is to lessen the risk by aiming for the center of the court to give yourself the needed margin for error. Once again, the emphasis is on positive execution and not negative execution.

If you are nervous in a particular stage of a match, it would be impractical for me to give you reasons not to be nervous. Your body is feeling what it is feeling. You cannot control it. Besides, nervousness is not necessarily a bad thing. Remember to **aim conservatively with margin for error; do not actually hit the ball conservatively. Don't change the manner you have hit the ball in practice or previously in the match that allowed you to get to that point.** It is important for you to realize that your nerves are primarily a result of you allowing exterior stimuli into your thought processes. Be aware that they

can be distracting and try to get back to focusing on the present.
**Focus on the battle at hand and your current performance.
Get your thoughts away from the past or future (blown
chances, or winning/losing).**

TOURNAMENT HIGHLIGHTS: (Above) 11 year-old Mark Tija of Gainesville was the crowd favorite in tournament action this weekend. (Top, left) Bob Tuttle (Center) congratulates Division I runnerup David Desilets (left) and champion Mike Oransky (right) for their play. (Bottom, left) Tournament director Dolly Robinson (center) congraulates Women's Divison I runnerup (left) Betty Wachob and champion (right) Paula Rhoten. (Photos by Harvey Campbell)

above: This picture was taken from the Lake City Reporter in 1983. As a child, I routinely competed in both junior and adult events. This particular photo is from an adult tournament. I would often play and practice with adult opponents. I was looking for competition wherever I could find it. I used to live and die with every match. Every time I lost it felt like the end of the world, even in practice.

left: A picture of me with my lifelong friend, Mark Palus. When we were 14, we were awarded a one week scholarship to the Nick Bollettieri Tennis Academy. We were surprised to find the level of competition and instruction much weaker than we were expecting. (Nick was nowhere to be found).

right: Here I am sitting with the world's most well known tennis playing transsexual, Dr. Renee Richards. Periodically, she would practice at my club.

left: Battling as a youngster against an adult opponent.

below: This is me with my TCU coach, Bernard "Tut" Bartzen. Tut was a legend in his time going undefeated in Davis Cup play for the U.S. I am extremely grateful for the knowledge he provided me.

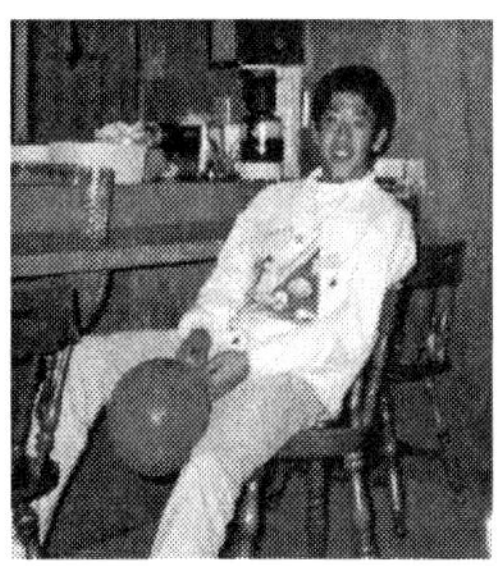

above: This picture was taken at the home of Coach Bartzen during my recruiting trip to TCU. Because I was a year ahead in school, I was only 16 at the time of this photo. Being young and physically immature, you can imagine the physical disadvantages I faced. When Coach Bartzen came to watch me play in a national tournament during the recruiting process, I lost 6-0, 6-0. Immediately after the match, he offered me a partial scholarship. Out of the many schools I was interested in, TCU was the only one to offer me a scholarship even though they were a top ten program.

above: Pictured here is the 1988-89 team during my freshman year at TCU which lost in the Final Four and finished the year at #4 in the country.
front row from left: Coach Bartzen, Jeff Giesea, Jeff Meyer, Mark Tjia, Luis Ruette, Gary Betts, Assistant Coach Karl Richter.
Back row from left: Tony Bujan, Mark van der Donk, Sandon Stolle, Clinton Banducci, Eric Lingg, Gerard Ronan.
Sandon is the son of tennis great, Fred Stolle. Sandon played #5 that year. Several years later, he went on to become #1 in the world in doubles.

above: Teaching ladies leagues at the 300 Club in Gainesville, FL.

below: Hitting a backhand during a
charity tournament in Gainesville,
Florida.

left: This picture was taken at a hotel in
Bangkok, Thailand. Shown here is another
former TCU teammate and doubles
partner, Ricardo Rubio. (You can see the
clothes that we washed by hand in the
bathroom sink in order to save money
hanging in the background)

Chapter Five

"COMPONENTS OF MATCH PLAY"

57

"Match management" is a term I use which describes the way a player conducts his or her match. This includes but is not limited to: concentration, strategy, knowledge of percentages, emotions, and momentum. The amount of concentration that it takes to excel at this game—that is, to consistently prevail in contests when your opponent is of similar physical ability—is extremely high. Most of us rarely require this kind of intensity in our daily activities. All you have to do is watch the professionals on TV to see examples of this intense concentration. It helps to develop rituals to help keep your focus. Many pros play with their strings to help keep themselves from inviting distractions. Try to avoid looking around too much. Everyone is different, but it is easy to find distraction if you go looking for it.

PLAYING WITH A LEAD

At the club level, I have many students who describe this exact scenario: "I was winning pretty easily, then I lost my concentration because things were going so well and before I knew it they had come back and I began to get nervous, causing me to play tentatively." Many times it is the same people telling me the same story time and time again. This is my perhaps overly simplistic response to them: "How many times must this happen to you before you finally understand that no lead is safe in this game? You can never take anything for granted."

Once upon a time, I knew the history of the scoring method in tennis. I no longer know it, because it is not really relevant to anything we are discussing. What is important is your acknowledgement that the scoring in tennis is designed to make the match close and competitive. It is designed to keep the losing player in the match until the very end. Yogi Berra, the former Hall of Fame manager of the New York Yankees, patented the quote, "It's never over 'til it's over." He could not have been more right, because in tennis as in baseball, there is no game clock. You must finish off your opponent. As long as you let your opponent linger in the match, he always has a chance until the last out is made or the last point won. Regardless of the size of the lead, the game is still in doubt until it is actually over. In baseball, you could be up by ten runs in the bottom of the ninth inning and need only one more out, and you could still lose the game. Likewise, in tennis, you could be up 6-0, 5-0 and still lose. It happens more often than you think. It has happened to me. In actuality, that may really only represent two breaks of serve. You cannot sit on the ball after you have built your lead as in other sports. You must finish your opponent off. Be very greedy with your points. Try to collect them all. If you were in a street fight for your life, when you knocked your assailant down, would you let him back up like the action heroes do in the movies? Of course not! You would pummel them until there was no chance they could get back up. That is the attitude you must have, as grim as that visual is.

In fact, in tennis, you could win the first set 6-0 and just be annihilating your opponent, and if he breaks your serve in the first game of the second set, you are technically already losing that set, even though you have won six games in the match and he has won only one. The fact that you were dominant in the first set has no relevance now. That was the past, and this is now the present. Your opponent has new life now. **The scoring in tennis is designed to make the match close, therefore allowing the mental game to make the difference. It is one of the few sports where you can actually win more points and games than your opponent and still lose the match.** Consider this; you lose 6-0, 6-7, 6-7 even though you have won 18 games to your opponent's 14.

THE TEN-POINT SUPER TIEBREAK

Many local leagues have adopted the ten-point super tiebreak to be played in lieu of a third set. This format, popular because of time constraints, actually emphasizes the mental game even more. By reducing the number of potential points played in the match, it is already an equalizer that favors the weaker opponent. Physical conditioning becomes less of a factor in the shortened format, obviously, but because fewer points are played, a difference in opponents' skill levels doesn't have as much time to play out. Chance plays a bigger role. This is one of the reasons why, in the major leagues and NBA playoffs, a best four out of seven series is played. They are trying to take the element of luck (such as a Hail Mary buzzer beater, or a bad call) out of the contest. If they played only one game to determine the winner, either team could win. In a best four out of seven, the better team will have more opportunities to let their advantages play out. Consider this: being the gambler that I am, I may sit down at a blackjack table and win my first ten hands. It is entirely possible, even though it has never happened to me. If I play well, the dealer only has about a 1 percent advantage over me. If I played only a few hands, that advantage would not be noticeable; there would not be enough time for it to significantly influence the outcome. However, the longer I play, the more that advantage begins to show, and that's when I begin to lose my money.

The point is, the longer you play, the more "true" the result. The same is true for tennis. A shortened match is an equalizer favoring the weaker opponent. In this format, points are more valuable. You cannot afford mental lapses, even short ones. Winning the first set in such a format is not all that significant an advantage. Remember that when you are down. Let's say for example that you and I are playing and you take the first set. Under the conventional format, you would need only one more set, while I would be looking at a daunting two more sets that I would need to win. In the shortened format, I would need only one more set, the same as you, plus a tiebreak to win. That is a pretty short sprint. For me, the loser of the first set, there is light at the end of the tunnel. The fact that you may have blanked me in the first set is of little relevance now, as we both need only one more set. Use this rationale to remind yourself to keep fighting when you are down and conversely to continue fighting when you are up.

USING YOUR EMOTIONS

The issue of emotions and the impact they may have on your performance is complicated because everyone reacts differently. People react differently because their personalities are different. As a coach of many junior and collegiate players, I have found myself coaching each player differently with regard to this topic. Generally, it is the rare person who plays better when angry or incited. Perhaps John McEnroe played better when there was some confrontation, usually with umpires. Sometimes I think he even sought it out in order to light a fire under him when he was flat. Many people think they play better when they are mad. It is my belief that most do not. Extended tantrums usually mean the plan is coming apart and panic is soon to follow. Showing positive emotion can be helpful, but negative emotion is usually detrimental and encouraging to your opponent. You should be aware of the signals you are sending to yourself and to your opponent. Do not underestimate the importance that positive and negative body language has on an opponent's psyche.

Some of my students play with no excitement or passion at all, and their play reflects that. With these students, I encourage grunting, fist pumping, leg slapping, etc. to show me and their opponents that they are not going away and are going to fight for the match. Lleyton Hewitt is a master at this, and he picks his moments well to get the crowd involved and thereby pump up his adrenaline to raise his level of play. As in other sports, adrenaline can boost your level of play and help you run down and hit shots you might not normally hit. In college tennis, I always loved to play the away matches where the crowds were antagonistic or even rude. It fired me up and I enjoyed instigating the crowd. It was not distracting to me and I played well in those conditions. I guess with my teammates there, it was kind of a gang mentality, which I enjoyed and can credit with pulling me through some matches. This is, after all, positive emotion I exhibited, celebrating good shots and not animating the bad ones.

However, relying on adrenaline can also be dangerous, as I learned once I finished college and took that mentality to the pros. The problem with emotional highs is that you usually set yourself up for some kind of low as well. You can't maintain that jacked-up emotional energy the entire time. In college tennis, you only have to play one match every couple of days. You can afford to get jacked up. In individual tournaments, you have to play five or six matches in a week in order to win the tournament. I quickly learned to curb the emotional outbursts and use them selectively. If I won a tough emotional match, I found I did not have much left for the next day and would come out flat or emotionally drained. I learned to take more of a businesslike approach to tournaments, trying to use positive emotional outbursts only to get me through very close situations such as a third set tiebreaker. My advice to those of you who play better with the fist-pumping stuff is to pick and choose your moments. Remember that this is a game that requires touch, deft timing, balance, and strategy. It is not a game of pure speed and brute power, and unmanaged adrenaline can often lead to over-hitting.

LUCKY OPPONENTS

Ask any teaching pro and they will tell you about all the ridiculous things that their students say when they analyze their matches. That could be another book in itself. One of the more comical things I hear goes something like this: A student comes off the court having lost 6-0, 6-1 and proclaims that the match was really a lot closer than the score suggests. "Every game went to deuce." Does this sound vaguely familiar? When I hear stuff along these lines, I know that the student is taking this to mean that they were close in ability, almost insinuating that they were just a little unlucky to have not won more deuce games. That is a very positive outlook on the match, but maybe a little tainted. I tend to take a different approach to it, in the sense that such a match shows the large gap in mental skills between my student and their opponent. If they lose every close game, then that is not unlucky. It is no accident that their opponent wins every deuce game. It illustrates their opponent's superior mental skills to pull out every close game. My response to my students is that there is much more work to be done regarding their match management. They need to analyze why they were losing the close games instead of using it as an excuse to justify the lopsided score. The bottom line is if they are close in ability, they should not be getting spanked so badly.

CONFIDENCE

Confidence is such an abstract concept that seems so simple and important for success; however, it is very difficult to define or explain its impact. As a junior, I knew because I was told by parents and coaches that I needed confidence, but I wasn't sure exactly how it affected my play or how I was supposed to gain it. I couldn't understand how something as intangible as confidence could have such an impact on something as physical as hitting a tennis ball. Webster's defines confidence as "a state of mind or a manner marked by easy coolness and freedom from uncertainty." That freedom from uncertainty means having no doubt about your ability to achieve a particular task. For instance, when you're hitting that second serve at match point, the thought that you might not be successful doesn't even enter your mind. You know you will make it; no doubt. Even when you do fail, if you are a confident person, you will consider that failure to be a fluke and will not doubt yourself in a similar situation next time. They say that "success breeds confidence," and this is true, but how do you get success without first having confidence? The answer is from practice. You cannot bluff confidence. You cannot suddenly tell yourself to go after that second serve at match point and that you are suddenly confident, when you haven't hit hundreds of those serves in practice. Having had success in practice gives you the reassurance when it comes time to produce in the match.

As I stated earlier, satellites consist of four separate tournaments, each lasting a week. It's always the same people from week to week within each individual satellite. On two separate satellites, the same thing happened to me. In the second week of the very first complete satellite I ever played, I was scheduled to play a fellow by the name of Mark Draper. Mark had won week one of the satellite and was the second or third seed here. As this was my initial foray into professional tennis, I was a bit intimidated. I guess I figured he was a much better and more experienced player than me, and I sort of expected that I would probably lose. Well, things went as expected, as I didn't offer much resistance in losing 6-2, 6-1. That is not to say that I did not try. I tried very hard, but I just did not expect to fare very well. I think I would have been happy to just not get blown off the court and embarrassed. That was my intent, but your intent is always supposed to be on winning. Anyhow, I came off the court feeling unimpressed with his game. He was certainly beatable. I was disappointed with myself for giving him too much credit. I felt unfulfilled and empty. Two weeks later in week four of the same satellite, I drew him again in the second round of the masters. This time, I had no fear because I believed that if I played well, I had a legitimate chance to win. As I began winning the first set, my belief or confidence grew and I proceeded to win the match by the exact same score: 6-2, 6-1. In a satellite in Indonesia, I made the exact same mistake when I lost to first-week winner Mahesh Bhupathi of India 6-2, 6-1, only to beat him ten days later 6-2, 6-1. I will always remember these matches because of the exact reversal of score and because of the way I felt after the first time I played them. These examples show the power of confidence and belief. On very few occasions have I won matches when I didn't think I would. Usually when I don't believe I can win, I get beaten pretty soundly. On those few occasions where I didn't, it was because sometime during the match, my opponents gave me the belief that I could win by letting me hang around for too long. Had they jumped out to quick starts to let me know I didn't belong, I would have gone away with a whimper.

We have a tendency to put labels on people and to try to predict outcomes in our society. Every sports show has a panel of experts picking winners and losers of sporting events with lots of analysis and statistics to prove their theories. As a player, you must be careful not to do that. Don't label people as seeded, strong players, weak players, ranked players, etc. I remember when I first started playing tournaments at eight years of age; I would evaluate my chances of winning my match when I met my opponent at the tournament desk. I would look to see how far he had come to play the tournament. The farther he came, the lesser my chances, I figured. If he was a foreigner, especially Hispanic, then I had no chance. I would look to see how nice his clothes were (if it was Fila or Ellesse then I was toast) or how many rackets he had. It sounds silly now, but we still do that type of thing. What is my opponent seeded? Who did he just beat? If he beats Ralph and Ralph beats me, then what chance do I have? I did well in algebra. Sports don't work that way. When I talk to club players, they seem to assume that the better player will always win the match. They figure that since they beat Tom yesterday, they will always beat him. It is not that simple; that is why we play the match. Don't put labels or expectations on people. Just perform. It doesn't matter who your opponent is or what they have done. I remember I used to hope I wouldn't have to play certain people for one reason or another, whether it was because they were my friend or because of their style of play. Don't get into thinking like that, because you probably will play them and you don't want to have any apprehension about that. The opponent matters not in how well you perform.

Let me warn you, too, about underestimating opponents. My worst losses stemmed from stepping onto the court cocky, believing there was no way I could lose. I rarely ever get overconfident because I usually underestimated my ability, as I illustrated earlier. However, one of my biggest mistakes as a player came in a challenger in Singapore in 1994. Due to my limited funds, my chances to make the jump to the next level from satellites were very limited. I would be given few opportunities to produce. In the first round of qualifying, I beat Andres Vysand, ranked #297 in the world and formally a top 100 player, which was my biggest-ranking win at the time. I beat Andres in the morning in a tough three-setter and was scheduled to play the second and final round of qualifying later that afternoon. I had an opportunity to watch my opponent play his first-round match, and I came away unimpressed. He looked out of shape for a professional, his strokes were awkward, his ranking was low, and I had never heard of him before. During lunch, several guys who knew him expressed their confidence to me that I would have no problems beating him. I listened to them too much and began believing that there was no chance I could lose. After all, I had been playing well, coming off one of the biggest wins of my life. In addition, I had better physical skills, as witnessed by myself and by others. Normally I get nervous before matches, but before this match I was uncharacteristically calm and **dangerously comfortable**. In fact, I was already thinking ahead to what competing in the main draw might be like. I proceeded to get beaten in straight sets before I could even blink. As it was happening I was in denial, laughing off the great shots he had made as if it was luck. But it wasn't luck. He had beaten me soundly, and I had lost out on a great opportunity because of my cockiness. In summary, I had one of my biggest victories and worst losses in the same day. This just proves my point of the impact your state of mind has on your game. It is not good to be too comfortable on the court during the match. You need to feel some uneasiness and wariness at your opponent's ability no matter how easy things are going at the time. **Always respect everyone's ability to defeat you, but never give anyone too much respect.**

GREED IS GOOD

In Gainesville, where I teach tennis, we have a Women's Day League where teams from the different facilities compete against other teams at their level (NTRP 3.0, 3.5, and 4.0). The number of matches that go to third sets is alarming. It is not the fact that the matches go to three sets that makes it worth noting because the ladies are, after all, grouped by ability and therefore relatively compatible with regard to their physical skills. Time and time again, a team will win a competitive first set, take a short break for cheese and crackers (an odd Gainesville League tradition), and then, breathing a sigh of relief, come out slightly complacent in the start of the second set, as if the beginning of the second set is somehow less important than the end of the first.

It doesn't take much to shift momentum the other way. Once the ball is rolling in your opponent's direction, it can be very difficult to stop. I cannot stress enough the importance of being greedy with your points and games. Matches consist of swings in momentum. The challenge lies in minimizing your opponent's swings and prolonging your own. If you are up 5-0, don't throw your opponent a bone by being content to allow them a game. Don't give them anything to build on. **Be greedy**! If they earn that game, that is one thing, but make sure they earn it and you don't concede it. This greedy mindset occurs naturally in some, but most of us need to make a conscious effort to be relentlessly focused on the task at hand until completion. Remember that tennis is combative, with one victor and one victim. Don't be the victim. To steal a quote from Gordon Gecko in the movie *Wall Street,* "Greed is good."

One of the pros at a facility across town, the late Jillian Alexander, used to joke with me about how we should start our teams' matches in the third set, knowing that many of our ladies teams would follow this formula and end up battling out a third set, regardless of which team won the first.

FEAR OF LOSING

To really be successful at achieving your potential, **you must always strive for perfection, but learn to accept that disappointment is a part of competition**. Learning to deal with disappointment is an important part of your growth as a competitor. Do not let it devastate you. Find the positives and negatives when evaluating your performance after a match. Both are always present. You will never play a match where you do everything right, but you will also never play a match where you do everything wrong either. You must learn to accept defeat and disappointment. Learn from them, but then let go of them. If you cling to disappointments for too long, they can haunt you incessantly. If you carry your losses with you, it can add unnecessary pressure for you in future similar situations. For example, say you lose a heartbreaker in a third set tiebreaker after having match points. Those kinds of matches can tear at your heart. You must learn to forget them or else perhaps next time you are in a similar situation, you may begin to doubt or think negatively about not repeating the same outcome instead of playing in the moment.

If you play tennis often enough, you are going to have lots of losses. If you don't, you either have a great mental game, in which case I don't know why you are reading this book, or you are playing out of level. Translation: You are not playing anybody any good. If two opponents play the match of their lives, someone is still going to lose, even in the pros. If you look at the year-to-date records of pros ranked 70 in the world and lower, they will all have either .500 or losing records. Consider this: one of the biggest tournaments in the world, the U.S. Open, begins with 128 of the best players in the world competing for one title. Only one person, the champion, leaves undefeated. Sixty-four players will lose in the first round and leave 0-1. Another 32 players will lose in the second round and leave 1-1. So in other words, out of the 128 that start the tournament, only 32 players leave with a winning record.

The point is, losing is a part of competing. **Losses should only motivate you, not discourage you**. If you use your hatred or distaste for losing as a motivator, that is a mark of a winner, but if you let your hatred of losing lead to a fear of losing, or rather, an unwillingness to deal with the possible heartache and disappointment, it is likely that your effort could suffer. You may rationalize to yourself, consciously or unconsciously, that it is less hurtful to get beat soundly knowing you did not give it your best than to get your heart broken from a hard-fought, gut-wrenching loss. To quote one of my favorite musicians, Billy Joel, "some people stay far away from the door if there is a chance of it opening up." That is not a good mindset for athletics, and believe me, I speak from experience.

ERROR MANAGEMENT

Included in match management is the concept of "error management." One of the common errors players make at the club level is not knowing how to play the percentages in order to manage their errors more efficiently. One of my coaches from my junior days, Andi Brandi (ex-University of Florida women's coach and current coach of touring pro Lisa Raymond) stated it perfectly: "A high-percentage player understands that tennis is a game of errors. The primary objective in tennis at any level will never change. Stroke the ball over the net and keep the ball well inside the lines-one more time than your opponent." (*Florida Tennis*, "High-Percentage Tennis Wins," September 2004. page 28). It is my assertion that you are more likely to win a point from your opponent's mistake than you will from your own winner. For you impatient players, realize that you do not always have to "win" your points; your opponent will lose plenty of them for you if you give them enough opportunities. Hence my advice earlier to hit your ball well, like you do in practice, but be conservative in your targets. My whole life, coaches and parents alike stressed how the professionals hit the ball so deep, within a foot or two of the baseline every time. This is untrue. Have you ever closely watched on TV where the balls are actually landing? Many balls—rather, the majority of balls—land well inside the court, often just past or even in front of the service line. However, they are hit with so much pace and topspin that it is not easy to take advantage of those balls. Take for instance the following statistics from the 2004 French Open (from www.RolandGarros.com):

> MATCH STATISTICS

Carlos Moya ESP (5)   0   5   6³   3

Guillermo Coria ARG (3)   ✓   0   7   7⁷   6

> DRAWS

Elapsed Time by Set: 50   55 40

	Moya (ESP)	Coria (ARG)
1st Serve %	54 of 115 = 47 %	72 of 98 = 73 %
Aces	3	2
Double Faults	5	5
Unforced Errors	56	26
Winning % on 1st Serve	38 of 54 = 70 %	49 of 72 = 68 %
Winning % on 2nd Serve	22 of 61 = 36 %	13 of 26 = 50 %
Winners (Including Service)	37	27
Receiving Points Won	36 of 98 = 37 %	55 of 115 = 48 %
Break Point Conversions	4 of 6 = 67 %	7 of 10 = 70 %
Net Approaches	17 of 33 = 52 %	15 of 20 = 75 %
Total Points Won	96	117
Fastest Serve	208 km/h	187 km/h
Average 1st Serve Speed	188 km/h	152 km/h
Average 2nd Serve Speed	134 km/h	134 km/h

> MATCH STATISTICS

Gustavo Kuerten BRA (28)   0   2 6 4 6⁶

David Nalbandian ARG (8) ✔ 0   6 3 6 7⁸

> DRAWS

Elapsed Time by Set: 40 38 42   68

	Kuerten (BRA)	Nalbandian (ARG)
1st Serve %	71 of 133 = 53 %	72 of 121 = 60 %
Aces	9	5
Double Faults	3	7
Unforced Errors	68	46
Winning % on 1st Serve	48 of 71 = 68 %	47 of 72 = 65 %
Winning % on 2nd Serve	26 of 62 = 42 %	26 of 49 = 53 %
Winners (Including Service)	51	39
Receiving Points Won	48 of 121 = 40 %	59 of 133 = 44 %
Break Point Conversions	6 of 13 = 46 %	8 of 15 = 53 %
Net Approaches	22 of 36 = 61 %	23 of 36 = 64 %
Total Points Won	122	132
Fastest Serve	195 km/h	190 km/h
Average 1st Serve Speed	172 km/h	161 km/h
Average 2nd Serve Speed	137 km/h	142 km/h

Match Completed

Gaston Gaudio ARG ✓   0   6   6   6
Lleyton Hewitt AUS (12)   0   3   2   2

Elapsed Time by Set: 39   36   41

	Gaudio (ARG)	Hewitt (AUS)
1st Serve %	39 of 73 = 53 %	45 of 85 = 53 %
Aces	1	2
Double Faults	1	5
Unforced Errors	19	43
Winning % on 1st Serve	23 of 39 = 59 %	23 of 45 = 51 %
Winning % on 2nd Serve	24 of 34 = 71 %	16 of 40 = 40 %
Winners (Including Service)	27	21
Receiving Points Won	46 of 85 = 54 %	26 of 73 = 36 %
Break Point Conversions	7 of 14 = 50 %	2 of 3 = 67 %
Net Approaches	20 of 21 = 95 %	18 of 31 = 58 %
Total Points Won	93	65
Fastest Serve	188 km/h	190 km/h
Average 1st Serve Speed	161 km/h	169 km/h
Average 2nd Serve Speed	132 km/h	136 km/h

> MATCH STATISTICS

Tim Henman GBR (9)   ✓ 0   6 6 6
Juan Ignacio Chela ARG (22) 0   2 4 4

> DRAWS

Elapsed Time by Set: 31 45 34

	Henman (GBR)	Chela (ARG)
1st Serve %	52 of 87 = 60 %	50 of 78 = 64 %
Aces	3	3
Double Faults	2	2
Unforced Errors	28	10
Winning % on 1st Serve	38 of 52 = 73 %	33 of 50 = 66 %
Winning % on 2nd Serve	21 of 35 = 60 %	14 of 28 = 50 %
Winners (Including Service)	42	19
Receiving Points Won	31 of 78 = 40 %	28 of 87 = 32 %
Break Point Conversions	5 of 9 = 56 %	1 of 5 = 20 %
Net Approaches	49 of 68 = 72 %	11 of 24 = 46 %
Total Points Won	90	75
Fastest Serve	193 km/h	180 km/h
Average 1st Serve Speed	176 km/h	164 km/h
Average 2nd Serve Speed	148 km/h	140 km/h

> MATCH STATISTICS

Guillermo Coria ARG (3)	✓	0	3	6	6	7
Tim Henman GBR (9)		0	6	4	0	5

> DRAWS

Elapsed Time by Set: 35 48 30 54

	Coria (ARG)	Henman (GBR)
1st Serve %	79 of 114 = 69 %	59 of 116 = 51 %
Aces	0	2
Double Faults	4	5
Unforced Errors	18	43
Winning % on 1st Serve	49 of 79 = 62 %	38 of 59 = 64 %
Winning % on 2nd Serve	17 of 35 = 49 %	21 of 57 = 37 %
Winners (Including Service)	24	46
Receiving Points Won	57 of 116 = 49 %	48 of 114 = 42 %
Break Point Conversions	9 of 13 = 69 %	5 of 11 = 45 %
Net Approaches	16 of 26 = 62 %	43 of 79 = 54 %
Total Points Won	123	107
Fastest Serve	182 km/h	200 km/h
Average 1st Serve Speed	156 km/h	176 km/h
Average 2nd Serve Speed	137 km/h	142 km/h

> MATCH STATISTICS   David Nalbandian ARG (8)   0   3 6^5 0

> DRAWS   **Gaston Gaudio** ARG   ✓   0   6 7^7 6

Elapsed Time by Set: 41 79 26

	Nalbandian (ARG)	Gaudio (ARG)
1st Serve %	74 of 114 = 65 %	42 of 82 = 51 %
Aces	2	1
Double Faults	5	1
Unforced Errors	46	19
Winning % on 1st Serve	37 of 74 = 50 %	27 of 42 = 64 %
Winning % on 2nd Serve	15 of 40 = 38 %	22 of 40 = 55 %
Winners (Including Service)	37	27
Receiving Points Won	33 of 82 = 40 %	62 of 114 = 54 %
Break Point Conversions	4 of 9 = 44 %	9 of 16 = 56 %
Net Approaches	13 of 22 = 59 %	14 of 19 = 74 %
Total Points Won	85	111
Fastest Serve	182 km/h	187 km/h
Average 1st Serve Speed	153 km/h	158 km/h
Average 2nd Serve Speed	132 km/h	134 km/h

> MATCH STATISTICS

> DRAWS

		8	0	3	6	6
Gaston Gaudio ARG	✓	8	0	3	6	6
Guillermo Coria ARG (3)		6	6	6	4	1

Elapsed Time by Set: 67   24   37 53 30

	Gaudio (ARG)	Coria (ARG)
1st Serve %	99 of 149 = 66 %	89 of 136 = 65 %
Aces	2	5
Double Faults	9	6
Unforced Errors	55	54
Winning % on 1st Serve	57 of 99 = 58 %	46 of 89 = 52 %
Winning % on 2nd Serve	23 of 50 = 46 %	22 of 47 = 47 %
Winners (Including Service)	36	38
Receiving Points Won	68 of 136 = 50 %	69 of 149 = 46 %
Break Point Conversions	11 of 15 = 73 %	11 of 23 = 48 %
Net Approaches	19 of 34 = 56 %	17 of 31 = 55 %
Total Points Won	148	137
Fastest Serve	187 km/h	187 km/h
Average 1st Serve Speed	164 km/h	147 km/h
Average 2nd Serve Speed	132 km/h	123 km/h

> MATCH STATISTICS

Anastasia Myskina RUS (6) ✔ 0   6   6
Venus Williams USA (4)   0   3   4

> DRAWS

Elapsed Time by Set: 28   45

	Myskina (RUS)	Williams (USA)
1st Serve %	40 of 65 = 62 %	32 of 55 = 58 %
Double Faults	2	4
Unforced Errors	13	43
Winning % on 1st Serve	29 of 40 = 73 %	21 of 32 = 66 %
Winning % on 2nd Serve	13 of 25 = 52 %	7 of 23 = 30 %
Winners (Including Service)	9	12
Receiving Points Won	27 of 55 = 49 %	23 of 65 = 35 %
Break Point Conversions	4 of 6 = 67 %	2 of 8 = 25 %
Net Approaches	3 of 3 = 100 %	7 of 11 = 64 %
Total Points Won	69	51
Fastest Serve	166 km/h	182 km/h
Average 1st Serve Speed	137 km/h	158 km/h
Average 2nd Serve Speed	113 km/h	129 km/h

> MATCH STATISTICS

Paola Suarez ARG (14)   ✓   0   6   6
Maria Sharapova RUS (18)   0   1   3

> DRAWS

Elapsed Time by Set: 26 33

	Suarez (ARG)	Sharapova (RUS)
1st Serve %	21 of 40 = 53 %	23 of 46 = 50 %
Double Faults	4	6
Unforced Errors	10	40
Winning % on 1st Serve	14 of 21 = 67 %	8 of 23 = 35 %
Winning % on 2nd Serve	9 of 19 = 47 %	6 of 23 = 26 %
Winners (Including Service)	5	11
Receiving Points Won	32 of 46 = 70 %	17 of 40 = 43 %
Break Point Conversions	7 of 9 = 78 %	3 of 4 = 75 %
Net Approaches	0 of 1 = 0 %	5 of 8 = 63 %
Total Points Won	55	31
Fastest Serve	161 km/h	172 km/h
Average 1st Serve Speed	152 km/h	153 km/h
Average 2nd Serve Speed	140 km/h	140 km/h

Jennifer Capriati USA (7) ✔	6	6	2	6
Serena Williams USA (2)	3	3	6	3

Elapsed Time by Set: 36   35   29 36

	Capriati (USA)	Williams (USA)
1st Serve %	52 of 80 = 65 %	45 of 84 = 54 %
Double Faults	1	5
Unforced Errors	24	45
Winning % on 1st Serve	35 of 52 = 67 %	28 of 45 = 62 %
Winning % on 2nd Serve	13 of 28 = 46 %	18 of 39 = 46 %
Winners (Including Service)	12	19
Receiving Points Won	38 of 84 = 45 %	32 of 80 = 40 %
Break Point Conversions	5 of 8 = 63 %	4 of 14 = 29 %
Net Approaches	9 of 11 = 82 %	5 of 10 = 50 %
Total Points Won	86	78
Fastest Serve	179 km/h	185 km/h
Average 1st Serve Speed	150 km/h	161 km/h
Average 2nd Serve Speed	124 km/h	129 km/h

| > MATCH STATISTICS | Amelie Mauresmo FRA (3) | | 0 | 4 | 3 |
| > DRAWS | **Elena Dementieva** RUS (9) | ✓ | 0 | 6 | 6 |

Elapsed Time by Set: 46 47

	Mauresmo (FRA)	Dementieva (RUS)
1st Serve %	45 of 68 = 66 %	37 of 61 = 61 %
Double Faults	3	7
Unforced Errors	33	29
Winning % on 1st Serve	21 of 45 = 47 %	22 of 37 = 59 %
Winning % on 2nd Serve	10 of 23 = 43 %	11 of 24 = 46 %
Winners (Including Service)	18	27
Receiving Points Won	28 of 61 = 46 %	37 of 68 = 54 %
Break Point Conversions	4 of 8 = 50 %	7 of 14 = 50 %
Net Approaches	9 of 14 = 64 %	15 of 19 = 79 %
Total Points Won	59	70
Fastest Serve	166 km/h	166 km/h
Average 1st Serve Speed	152 km/h	142 km/h
Average 2nd Serve Speed	132 km/h	128 km/h

Paola Suarez ARG (14)   0   0   5

Elena Dementieva RUS (9)   ✓   0   6   7

Elapsed Time by Set: 27 57

	Suarez (ARG)	Dementieva (RUS)
1st Serve %	31 of 57 = 54 %	33 of 62 = 53 %
Double Faults	8	9
Unforced Errors	39	30
Winning % on 1st Serve	14 of 31 = 45 %	19 of 33 = 58 %
Winning % on 2nd Serve	6 of 26 = 23 %	11 of 29 = 38 %
Winners (Including Service)	10	15
Receiving Points Won	32 of 62 = 52 %	37 of 57 = 65 %
Break Point Conversions	4 of 8 = 50 %	8 of 13 = 62 %
Net Approaches	1 of 2 = 50 %	6 of 8 = 75 %
Total Points Won	52	67
Fastest Serve	158 km/h	164 km/h
Average 1st Serve Speed	145 km/h	148 km/h
Average 2nd Serve Speed	136 km/h	118 km/h

Anastasia Myskina RUS (6) ✓	0	6	6
Jennifer Capriati USA (7)	0	2	2

Elapsed Time by Set: 30 31

	Myskina (RUS)	Capriati (USA)
1st Serve %	27 of 56 = 48 %	37 of 57 = 65 %
Double Faults	3	1
Unforced Errors	29	36
Winning % on 1st Serve	21 of 27 = 78 %	20 of 37 = 54 %
Winning % on 2nd Serve	16 of 29 = 55 %	6 of 20 = 30 %
Winners (Including Service)	17	11
Receiving Points Won	31 of 57 = 54 %	19 of 56 = 34 %
Break Point Conversions	5 of 11 = 45 %	1 of 4 = 25 %
Net Approaches	6 of 7 = 86 %	4 of 6 = 67 %
Total Points Won	68	45
Fastest Serve	166 km/h	166 km/h
Average 1st Serve Speed	145 km/h	137 km/h
Average 2nd Serve Speed	113 km/h	120 km/h

> **MATCH STATISTICS**   Elena Dementieva RUS (9)   0   1   2

> **DRAWS**   **Anastasia Myskina** RUS (6)   ✓   0   6   6

Elapsed Time by Set: 28 31

	Dementieva (RUS)	Myskina (RUS)
1st Serve %	21 of 45 = 47 %	35 of 56 = 63 %
Aces	1	0
Double Faults	10	5
Unforced Errors	33	17
Winning % on 1st Serve	11 of 21 = 52 %	26 of 35 = 74 %
Winning % on 2nd Serve	8 of 24 = 33 %	10 of 21 = 48 %
Winners (Including Service)	11	12
Receiving Points Won	20 of 56 = 36 %	26 of 45 = 58 %
Break Point Conversions	1 of 3 = 33 %	5 of 8 = 63 %
Net Approaches	5 of 9 = 56 %	2 of 3 = 67 %
Total Points Won	39	62
Fastest Serve	164 km/h	164 km/h
Average 1st Serve Speed	148 km/h	137 km/h
Average 2nd Serve Speed	126 km/h	112 km/h

I have included the statistics of the eight men's and women's quarterfinal matches, all four semis, and both finals to illustrate the impact of unforced errors on the outcome of a match. The results after analyzing the numbers are quite interesting. Remember that these statistics included men and women of varying styles of play. Included are fourteen total matches, seven from the men and seven from the ladies' draws. In these matches, the player with the fewest unforced errors won twelve of the fourteen. The player with more winners only won six of the fourteen. That means in eight of those matches, the player with fewer winners actually won the match. In contrast, players who made more unforced errors than their opponents won only two matches. When you total the winners and unforced errors for all fourteen matches, it comes out like this:

Player who won match		Player who lost match	
Winners	**Unforced Errors**	**Winners**	**Unforced Errors**
319	363	341	589

As you can see, the players on the losing end of these matches hit 22 more winners than their opponents, but also committed 226 more unforced errors. I think it is safe to say that the numbers in the winners column are largely irrelevant, a sideshow if you will. Of far more importance are the numbers in the errors column.

All right, so the next question is: How do we reduce our mistakes? Well, being human, you will always make mistakes. It is unreasonable to expect to play an error-free match. However, it is not unreasonable to expect a player to play an error-free match with regard to concentration, effort, shot selection, and intent. A mentally aware player can achieve this even at the club level, thereby reducing their overall errors. Because strategy in doubles is basic, I even expect my club teams to not make errors in intent and shot selection regardless of their level. I can still hear Coach Bartzen at TCU hollering at us during practice about missing in the net when our opponent was at the baseline. Those were bad mistakes, as our goal was to hit deeper when our opponent was at the baseline. Because net clearance is directly relevant to depth, missing in the net meant that either our intent was wrong or we were way off our target, either of which was unacceptable. Missing in the net when our opponent is at the net is an acceptable mistake as we probably are trying to keep the ball fairly low to avoid an easy put-away volley. Other examples of unacceptable mistakes included missing a second serve or hitting a lob wide. A second serve would normally not travel fast enough to benefit from hitting it close to the sidelines. The same is true for a lob in that the depth and height of a lob is what is important, and not how close to the sideline it lands. A lob to the sidelines will not be any more advantageous than a lob of equal height and depth to the middle of the court.

An example of a mistake than can be both acceptable and unacceptable is playing balls that are going out. If a player is at the net or on the way to the net and he plays a ball that is headed out, that is actually an acceptable mistake. I could even applaud the decision to play the ball because it shows decisiveness. It is a judgment decision. When you are in doubt as to whether an opponent's shot is going to land in or out, it is always better to play it. In contrast, if you play a ball that is questionable and you are at the baseline, then that would be unacceptable because that is an error in your court awareness and not your judgment. You did not realize where you were standing, or you would not have played the ball. Good court awareness—knowing where everyone is on the court at all times, including yourself—can reduce total errors by identifying the high-percentage plays based on court positions. For example, in doubles, if I am aware of which opponent is closer to the net, I can determine where I want to hit my next ball. If I have a high volley or overhead (offensive shot), I would hit it at the closer player to the net, because he has less time to react to my hard shot. If I'm playing a neutral or defensive ball, I would play it to the player farther back, as it would be easier to keep it low and the baseline player's court position is obviously less offensive than his partner's.

Well then, how do you know where everyone is on the court if you are not ever supposed to take your eye off the ball?

You do this with the same skills and senses you use to know there is a car in the lane next to you while not ever taking your eye off the road: **awareness**. Your primary focus is always the ball; your peripheral focus is the court in front of you and your partner beside or behind you. **You must always know where everyone is on the court at all times, including yourself**. Court awareness is such an important factor in your decision making process, and good decisions will lead to overall fewer mistakes. Be very stingy with your unforced errors, that is, the number of free points you give to your opponent. Make your opponent earn the points he/she wins. Errors due to a lack of effort, concentration, or anger are all a result of a lack of discipline. They are avoidable, and therefore always unacceptable.

RISK ASSESSMENT

There are not a whole lot of things that I still remember from my marketing classes at TCU. One of the things I do remember is doing case analysis. One of the criteria we would use to determine if a course of action was wise or not was the risk associated with that action. This risk assessment weighted the benefits of a successful action to the negatives of an unsuccessful one. Being a gambler who periodically frequents Las Vegas, I make decisions on what to bet and how much to bet based on similar criteria. Playing percentage tennis involves the same skills. Taking risks in your shot selection may be necessary; however, there must be a significant benefit if the shot is successful. For example, in singles, when engaged in a cross-court rally with an opponent, the person who changes the direction of the ball is taking a risk. That in itself is not necessarily bad. If a player decides to take the ball down the line, the player must have the balance and court position to: 1) Be reasonably certain that he can be successful in changing the direction of the ball to hit down the line, over the highest part of the net and the shortest part of the court; and 2) Be sure that if successful, the shot has achieved something worthwhile, like putting an opponent on the defensive or off balance. Too often, I see players attempt to change direction from poor court positions simply because they are bored or impatient, therefore inviting unnecessary risk for very little benefit. How many of you would undertake that same strategy in the stock market, taking a large risk for a small potential gain? I don't think many of you would—at least I hope for your sake that you wouldn't—and if you did, you wouldn't for very long.

In doubles, when the net player poaches a ball, he is taking a risk. There is some inherent risk in making a poach; it is a calculated gamble. The opponent could drive the ball down the line, or angle the return out of the poacher's reach, or even lob over his head. As with anything else in life, with increased risk, there should be increased reward. The poacher should be close enough to the net so that **if** he gets his racket on the ball, he is virtually guaranteeing himself the opportunity to hit an unreturnable shot at the opposing net player. It makes no sense for the net player to take a risk and make a poach, but make it from so far away from the net that it is still difficult to put the ball away.

There should be rhyme and reason to your shots; every shot should have a specific intent. I am astounded at the number of times in a lesson I can stop the ball and ask a student what his intended target was, only to hear, "I don't know." If you cannot control the ball, that may say something about your skills or technique and the need perhaps for lessons or more practice, but if you can control the ball within reason and just don't think about what you want to do with it or where you want to put it, then that is unacceptable because your mind is on cruise control. That is setting the bar too low. Shoot for the A+ instead of merely a passing grade. If you have ball-control skills, use them on every ball. Don't get caught out there just slapping the ball around, content to just get it in the court. Until you can get to the point where your shots are intentional and relatively close to your intended target, you are not really playing tennis yet. Until that time, strategy and anticipation are not really all that useful. If you are just poking the ball around hoping that it goes somewhere "good," then don't be surprised if it doesn't.

In my clinics, players will hit unintentional shots that happen to be winners and will get the congratulatory "good shot" from the opponent, when in reality it is really just blind luck. When playing billiards, how often do you hit a ball without knowing what ball and what pocket you are aiming at? If you happen to make a ball unintentionally, it is common etiquette to either take that ball out of the pocket or at least cede your turn. I believe the terminology for such a shot in billiards is "junk." To say that your intent on every shot is absolutely necessary sounds like such an obvious statement, but you would be surprised the number of times players hit a ball with no real idea of where they are trying to go with it. I know I am.

BALL CONTROL

Having a specific intent with every shot is only the beginning. It doesn't do you very much good if you know where you want to hit your shot, but it just won't go there. Sound familiar? Ball control is one of the most overlooked aspects of good tennis. In order to deliberately control direction, depth, spin, and pace, you must have a good feel for the ball. I remember being a young whippersnapper, attending my very first soccer camp at what must have been seven or eight years of age. The camp was run by Mutlu Alper, one heck of a soccer player. Before we were allowed to learn anything else, we had to learn to be competent at juggling the soccer ball with our feet, thighs, chest, and head. This means we had to demonstrate body control, coordination, and touch before we were even allowed to start drills, much less scrimmage. You would be well served to demonstrate similar skills in tennis as well. This means being able to bounce the ball on the ground with your racket, picking up the ball with only your racket and no hands or feet, and bouncing the ball on your racket face without chasing it and stumbling around the complex like an undergrad during spring break. Too many people try to learn topspin and slice before ever learning ball and racket control. In trying to run before they can walk, these people are making the learning process much longer and more frustrating for both themselves and their coach (that would be me and people like me). The racket is to a player what a brush is to a painter; you are creating shots out there, not clubbing something to death.

Once you have demonstrated reasonable control, you can then proceed with technique. Form and technique are so important in this game. You can only advance so far without proper technique, but technique alone without proper "feel" won't get you very far either. Technique can be taught by a third party such as an instructor, but "feel" can only really be self-learned. As a career instructor, I have not yet found a way to teach "feel." I believe that in order to teach yourself feel, you must train and play with conscious targets. I am talking about extremely specific targets, not just general areas of the court. For example, mark off an area of the court; say a circle with a five-foot radius. Try to hit your shots in that circle by evaluating and adjusting your shot every time you miss. Try not to make the same mistake twice in a row. If you miss three feet short of the circle, try not to miss the next ball short again. If you hit in the center, remember how that felt and try to clone that shot on the next ball. Aspire to be like a machine. If you train with this mentality, you can literally learn from every ball you hit. Just think, you could easily hit 500-1000 balls in an hour, and by learning from each of those, you could really improve your "feel" in a short amount of time. This has little to do with technique. I have seen many a player consumed with executing great technique but with very little control over where the ball was actually going, as if somehow proper technique alone would magically make their shots winners. In contrast, I have seen club players with technique that would make you cringe, and yet they continually put the ball on a dime.

Technique matters greatly, but it is not the only thing that matters, especially in club play. I like to draw comparisons to my poor basketball-playing ability. I am a reasonably good athlete and without having any formal basketball experience, I can look like Kobe Bryant when shooting, but I can't put the ball in the hoop with any kind of regularity. My form is flawless, but my feel is not there because I haven't shot enough. When shooting a basketball, most people consciously make ongoing corrections to their shot. In other words, if they shoot an air ball short of the rim, usually the next shot will not also be an air ball. Can you imagine yourself practicing your jump shot without an intended target, the basket? Of course you wouldn't. How would you know if your shot went where you wanted it to go? Yet I see people hit balls all the time with the intent simply to just get it in. When you throw a dart at a dartboard, you throw at an intended target, usually the bull's-eye. You aren't happy with just hitting the board or the wall. After seeing where the first dart landed, you can then make an adjustment to your next throw. This is the process by which you learn "feel," through trial and error. It is no different in tennis. It requires a distinct target, the bull's-eye or a reference point, from which to make an adjustment on your next shot.

Often when teaching clinics, I do drills where students are required to keep the ball in a particular part of the court, such as playing out points using only half a court. Adults and kids alike have so much trouble keeping the ball in such a small court. This failure demonstrates either a lack of intent or a lack of ball control. People, however, will justify it by claiming that they are used to hitting the ball to an open court and that is why they failed to keep it in the designated half. To this, my reply is "BS." No one is conditioned to automatically hit shots to an open court as if it is a reflex they cannot control. If you can control a ball to a particular part of the court or a person, then you can also control it to an open court if you so desire. That is how it works, only through deliberate intent. Anything else is just dumb luck. If you are one of those people who has trouble warming up because you cannot hit the ball to your opponent, recognize that your ball control leaves something to be desired. Do not convince yourself that once the match begins you will suddenly be able to control the ball as you desire. For instance, if you hit a perfect lob winner in your match, but you did not intend to hit a lob, I am not so sure you should be feeling all that good about it even though you may have just looked like a superstar. Remember to always try to make the ball go where you want with deliberate intent. Don't just hit and hope. This is akin to buying a ticket for the lottery.

MOMENTUM

Momentum, like confidence, is an intangible concept that can have such a dramatic impact on the outcome of a match. The two are in fact very closely related, with one giving life to the other. In other sports, particularly basketball, a team can quickly gain momentum in a game (usually with the help of the crowd), hitting a stretch where everything is going right. It is almost as if the entire team has just been given a temporary injection of confidence, and the team plays without fear of failure or doubt of success. This is usually the time when the opposing team will take a time-out, if only to just break the momentum. This temporary lull settles down the crowd and the players just long enough so they have time to think, maybe even doubt, but certainly not to just keep reacting.

In pro tennis, more and more frequently, players are taking injury time-outs more to quell an opponent's momentum than to tend to a serious injury. It is happening often enough to warrant talk of changing the injury time-out rule. It is quite an effective strategy, though reeking of gamesmanship if you ask me. There are other more ethical ways to break an opponent's momentum.

You can disrupt the rhythm of the match by mixing in off-speed shots such as slices or lobs. Take a little more time in between points and games, staying within the rules of course. Following this logic, rain delays or other stoppages in play tend to favor the player who is losing. On the other side of the coin, if momentum is in your favor, try to continue playing at the pace you are on. The bottom line is that in a match between two compatible opponents, there will inevitably be swings in momentum for both sides. The challenge is to keep the shifts in your direction long while keeping your opponent's short. That means that when riding a 5-0 lead in the first set, try to keep this momentum going by working hard for that particular game. Don't see it as a cushion where games are not as important. A 6-0 set as opposed to a 6-1 or 6-2 set sends a different message to both you and your opponent heading into the second set.

EXCUSES

This is one of the most important and one of my personal favorite topics to discuss because as a coach I hear it so much. I hear excuses from people who don't even know they are giving me excuses about why they played badly or why they lost. When a student comes to me and begins a sentence with "I don't want to make excuses, **but**…" what they really mean to say is, "Take out a pencil and paper to take dictation, because here they come." I have heard it all ranging from "not enough sleep" to "broken strings" to "bad partners" to "I didn't feel like playing." Well, you get the point. In fact, I have heard so many excuses that I could write a whole other book on just that subject alone. Making excuses for yourself is really a reflection of a lack of true self-confidence and can easily become habit forming. Remember how we discussed earlier that it takes a big person to shake hands with their opponent and acknowledge that they were out-prepared and out-played that day? When you make excuses, you are not really acknowledging that. That oversight is harmful to your overall development and improvement as a player, not to mention the fact that it is not a stellar example of fine sportsmanship. People, even your friends and especially your coach (i.e. me), do not want to hear excuses. You don't have to verbalize your excuses for them to be detrimental. Even if you make them only to yourself, you are limiting your learning process as a player.

An excuse-driven mindset can be habit forming, even contagious. If you are not careful, you could easily find yourself making these excuses **during** the match, actually mentally preparing yourself for a loss while the outcome of the match is still being determined. There is no kind way of saying it, but the excuse-driven mindset is a **loser** mentality and has no place in the game. Nothing positive can come from it.

Players often return from tournaments or competitions describing how they played so well in one match only to play equally badly the next one. Sometimes this Jekyll/Hyde transformation can occur within the same day, literally in a matter of hours. Heck, I did it in Singapore in '94. Tell me if you have heard this one before: "I couldn't hit a ball in today."

There is no acceptable reason why your play should vary so much from day to day. **You must take responsibility for your own level of play**. Do not leave it up to fate as if you are waiting for the stars and planets to align correctly in order to determine if you will play well today. It is not out of your control. You and you alone control the quality of your own performance. When you have firmly grasped this concept, the excuse-driven mindset will be gone and so will the vast discrepancies in the quality of your play. You may still have days when you are a little sharper than others regarding your timing, movement, etc., but the differences should be minimal.

PREPARATION

Good preparation can go a long way toward eliminating many potential excuses. Good old Coach Bartzen at TCU made it known early on that he would not tolerate players being unprepared, whether that meant equipment, physical conditioning, mental toughness. He strongly suggested that we as players spend a few minutes directly before the match preparing ourselves mentally for the battle and the intense concentration that would be required to compete fiercely. Watching TV, reading a book, or wiping the sleep out of our eye was not his idea of ideal mental preparation. We were also expected to have all equipment ready. That meant **all** racket handles wrapped, rackets freshly strung (everyone who takes tennis seriously enough to be reading this book ought to have at least two rackets of the same make and of similar string tension), sweatbands, rosin, extra shirts, shorts, even extra contact lenses—basically everything that we might need with us—in our racket bag. Your bag is literally your survival kit. All this, and the clothes you plan to wear, should be thought out and packed the night before, when you are not distracted or rushed for time. Tennis is combative, remember? Would you go to a battle without everything you **might** need—your sword, helmet, armor, or shield?

"Preparation" encompasses many aspects. Hydrating yourself to help avoid heat exhaustion and cramping before a match is also solely your responsibility. I have a history of cramping, and since I know that about myself, I need to take extra precautions to make sure it has no impact on the outcome of my matches. My very first college match was in September 1988, in a tournament in Texarkana, Arkansas. If you have ever been to that part of the country at that time of year, you know how hot and humid it is. I was obviously extremely nervous and I think that the heat, the length of my match, and the tenacity of my Swedish opponent Mikael Gavelin, caused my troubles. Being young and inexperienced, I had not taken the precautionary measures to hydrate and prepare for the tough conditions. I paid for it. After the match, I went into a full-body cramp where it seemed every muscle of my body locked up at the same time. I literally cramped in every part of my body except maybe my forehead and ears. Let me tell you, it was a most unpleasant experience. I remember being carried by four or five of my teammates and rushed to the hospital, where I stayed the night having IVs dripped into me. That was a tough lesson to learn. It did not happen to directly impact that match, as I had already lost before I cramped. Had I won, however, I would obviously not have been able to continue on in the tournament. Since that day, I have become more wary of my preparedness. I eat bananas for potassium before and during my matches. The night before the match, I drink tomato juice (again for potassium), and lots of water. Hours before the match, I continue to drink lots of water until I can urinate clear. Only then am I confident of my status. During the match, it is more water, and I will usually sip on a bottle of Pedialyte (get the flavored kind, the original flavor tastes like sweat and is really quite repulsive; I don't know how babies drink that stuff). Everyone will tell you something different about how to properly hydrate. Some drink Gatorade or a similar type of sports drink. This is what works for me, and I thought I would share it. Whatever you do, prepare for the worst-case scenario.

Another important ingredient in preparing properly is warming up. Some people say they play better without warming up, and to that I say "BS" again. They are just being flat-out lazy. It is important to have broken a sweat before you step out on the court for your match. Your five- or ten-minute warm-up before you start playing is not enough. It is more cosmetic than anything else. At TCU, we would practice the day before at the facility where we were to play to get accustomed to the court surface. We would then come out for a hit in the morning for about an hour, and finally warm up again for 15 minutes an hour before the match. A warm-up should consist of hitting **every** stroke, and also playing out actual points. This is important not only to curtail injuries, but to make sure you are ready to go from the very first point. A good start or a bad one, for that matter, can be very difficult to overcome and could end up determining the whole match. Almost none of the young athletes I teach ever warm up for their tournament matches. As a lifetime veteran of tennis tournaments, I cannot understand that mentality. I was always at the site an hour early to stretch, warm up, go to the bathroom, and visualize my match. I personally needed to be in the tournament environment to set my tournament mindset and to get ready to compete. Every little detail, from bringing a comfortable hat to timing my meals, had to be planned out carefully in order for me to be able to compete distraction free. The game is hard enough as it is without having to worry about preventable distractions. All of this attention to detail regarding your preparation helps to illustrate the **discipline** required to be successful in competing in the art of tennis. You get what you put in. If you do not prepare to be successful, then you do not deserve to be.

Chapter Six

REVERSING A POOR PERFORMANCE

We have all had days where it seemed as if it was just not our day. A day where we are missing shots we normally wouldn't miss. Sometimes this occurs when we are forced to play under adverse conditions. It is important to have the proper mental approach when dealing with conditions on the court that are less than perfect. Always try to take a positive attitude when playing under these circumstances. Perfect playing conditions favor the "better" player. The worse the conditions are, the greater the equalizer. Try to win this mental battle in order to gain a competitive edge by taking a positive approach. Remember that conditions such as the weather, the court, the crowd, or whatever it may be are the same for both players. **The challenge here is to deal with these factors better than your opponent.** Do not let your opponent know that the wind or sun is bothering you or even that it affected you just for a fleeting moment. If you miss an overhead and then proceed to cuss at the sun, what do you think I am going to do the next time you come to the net? The worst thing you can do is take the "woe is me" approach and give your opponent ammunition in the mental warfare of this game. In college, we bitched incessantly about the wind during practice because our courts seemed to be set in some sort of wind tunnel, but during matches we loved it, as it was our opponents who were doing the bitching.

When playing poorly, do not lose sight of the fact that you and only you are responsible for your own level of play. Because of the scoring system that I discussed earlier, you are **never** out of it. It is always possible to turn around your level of play and possibly the outcome of the match. One of the most important lessons I try to relay to my young people is to never, ever give up. Always fight to the end. That mindset is what makes a person competitive, and that will earn you the respect of your peers and opponents, regardless of the outcome. That competitiveness can more than make up for a lack of talent, size, speed, power, youth, etc. Giving up during a match regardless of your talent makes you a **loser** in my book, literally. A true competitor would never do that; it goes against their nature.

Besides staying positive, there are a number of things you can do to help turn around a subpar performance. The most important is the movement of your feet. Chances are that you are not hitting the ball well because your timing is off, and timing starts with your feet. If you are nervous or tentative, the normal reaction is to quit moving. Remember this: Proper footwork entails more than just getting you from point A to point B. It also means achieving proper distance and rhythm. I once had a student ask me, "How do you know when to start your swing? Do you wait to see the ball at a certain point to know that it is time to swing?" I had to stop and think before answering, "No, I just feel it, I feel the rhythm," in much the same way a drummer feels the beat and reflexively pounds the canvas at the right time. He is not counting beats in his head (one, two, three, smack) like he might have when he was first learning. What is rhythm in tennis and how do you achieve it? It is exactly as it is in music, and you achieve it through movement and sound.

Coach Tut Bartzen once told me that when he was a young man, his coach could be blindfolded with his back to the court and could tell whether Tut was hitting a forehand or backhand. Many thought it was a parlor trick, but it was no trick. His coach simply listened to the time interval—that is, the slight difference in the time that elapsed between the sound of the ball hitting the court and to the sound of the ball hitting the strings. You see, Tut hit the ball slightly longer after the bounce on his forehand than he did on his backhand. He played his forehand at the top of the bounce, while he played his backhand slightly before the crest. The key is he did it the same way **every** time. As a result, his coach could tell if Tut was hitting a forehand or backhand based solely on sound.

Because your opponent is not gracious enough to hit the ball in the same spot for you every time, it requires your movement into and away from the court to achieve a consistent time interval. I call this "taking and giving court." The next time you watch a match on television, take a piece of paper and cover up one half of the court. Just watch one player, and see how the player is constantly taking and giving court during baseline rallies. Sometimes, it is very subtle. Other times, it is so obvious the player might disappear from the screen. One shot might be hit from a yard inside the baseline, followed by a ball hit from a yard behind the baseline because his opponent had hit it slightly deeper. Players do not move just laterally across the baseline; they make slight adjustments in their movements, moving at angles, so they are able to play their ground strokes at a consistent time interval. You do not want to have to play one ball right after the bounce and the next well after the bounce. Your opponent will rarely cooperate with you in this regard, which means you have to move in order to give yourself a better chance at being successful by hitting the ball on your own terms. In other words, you are responsible for achieving your own rhythm. Do not rely on your opponent to create one for you. This rhythm actually includes the sound of your plant foot hitting the ground at the same time interval before the sound of you hitting the ball. Think about it. If I asked you to throw a ball, you would plant your foot and throw the ball with a consistent time interval without even thinking about it.

A common complaint I hear at the club level is that people have trouble playing against people who hit the ball with little pace. That just means you have to move to the ball more than you would with someone who hit the ball a little bit harder. The ball is not coming toward you anymore. **In order to be consistent, you have to hit the ball consistently.** This means having a consistent time interval between the ball bouncing, your foot planting, and the racket hitting the ball, and even the sound of your grunting. On ground strokes, you should have plenty of time to move to an area of the court that will allow you to hit the ball at your preferred time interval, providing you are on your toes and are carefully watching the ball come off your opponent's racket. After all, you do have some 70 feet from baseline to baseline within which to move only a few steps. In some cases, if you know how to hit with an open stance, only one or two steps are needed. In addition to their competitiveness and mental toughness, one of the major reasons Michael Chang and Lleyton Hewitt were able to rise to the elite of men's pro tennis was because of their speed and footwork. They are both extremely quick, which enables them to get to balls that other players cannot; but of far more importance and often overlooked is how they use their speed to hit balls on their own terms. Their movement allows them to set and hit balls at their preferred time intervals, enabling them to be consistent, accurate, and even powerful, given their diminutive size. In this way, they use their footwork as an advantage on every ball they hit and not just on the few balls where they make incredible gets. Footwork, along with the mental game, is a vastly underrated aspect of this game. Both are more important than your hard serve, the follow-through on your forehand, or the grip on your backhand. Less-than-perfect technique can be made up for by good movement and mental fortitude, especially at the recreational level.

In most sports, there is generally a positive connotation when you speak about aggressiveness. Tennis is no different. What does "aggressiveness" mean exactly? The answer is not clearly defined. It is very easy to confuse aggressiveness with going to the net, or hitting the ball 200 mph. It does not necessarily mean that. People play different styles, so it may mean different things for different people. For example, someone who is a counter-puncher is not supposed to be suddenly rushing the net at every opportunity. A simple universal definition of "aggressiveness" as it pertains to tennis is "moving to the ball and not waiting for the ball to come to you, hitting it with confidence and without fear." Notice the footwork and mental components of this definition.

CLOSING COMMENTS

When looking at notes that I wrote to myself during my time grinding away on the satellites, I found one of my observations in quotes and underlined. It read, **"A tennis match is life, summed up in a couple of hours."** I believe that there are many parallels between the struggles that you encounter in life and what you endure on the tennis court. There are ups and downs, trials and tribulations, great victories and bitter disappointments. It is how you deal with these ebbs and flows that determine whether you are a winner or a loser in life as on the court. Do you shy away from challenges? Does failure make you want to quit or does it make you more determined? Many of the millionaires in our society failed in their ventures many times over before finally succeeding.

Tennis is a fairly affluent sport. What I mean to say is most of the people that can afford to join a club, take tennis lessons, buy balls, and endure the many expenses that come with playing this sport are generally what I would consider fairly successful people. The qualities they possess to make them successful in society are the same qualities needed to achieve the same success on the tennis court: persistence, determination, performance under pressure, planning, discipline, focus, resilience, dealing with adversity. I could go on and on.

One of the primary benefits of getting young people involved in tennis is the life skills that it helps to develop. In order for junior players to achieve significant success on the court, they have to learn and demonstrate some of these qualities. The life skills that tennis teaches children are the same skills that adults have learned through their life experiences. Do you see the irony here? Children need to apply their skills learned from tennis to life, while adults need to apply their skills learned from life to their tennis. As an adult, do you worry about things you cannot control? Then why on the court do you worry about winning or losing when it is not completely under your control? The only thing that is under your total control is the quality of your performance. That is what you should be concerned about.

I hope that this book has been helpful to you, and maybe has helped to show you a perspective on the game that you may not have considered before. If it does not translate into improvement or increased enjoyment from the game, then at the very least, I hope it has provided you with some entertainment value. Remember to always **"Love the Battle"** more than the

reward. Good luck to you!